Service – How Do I Give
it means to live as a Christ
service are presented in an
profound ideas are made simple and then applied with punch.

Tim Chester
Pastor of Grace Church, Boroughbridge, Yorkshire
Faculty member with Crosslands Training
Author of several books

Christians often get 'stuck' in their spiritual growth, receiving from the church without giving back. This helpful book provides practical steps for believers – especially non-churched and/or newer believers – to overcome their hesitations, discover their spiritual gifts, and serve from a gospel motivation. For pastors who need help encouraging their people to serve the church, this is the first book I'd recommend.

Gavin Ortlund
Senior pastor, First Baptist Church, Ojai, California
author of *Theological Retrieval for Evangelicals*
and *Finding the Right Hills to Die On*

Service – How Do I Give Back? is a well-written, easy-to-grasp, comprehensive treatment of the 'all-in life' submission to which Jesus calls all His followers. The author seasons each chapter with narrative examples that allow readers to place themselves in the grand story of following King Jesus as His servant-disciples. This book is imminently practical, enjoyably readable, and pastorally helpful for making disciples and introducing people to Jesus.

Doug Logan, Jr.
Co-Director of Church in Hard Places with Acts 29
President of Grimké Seminary, Richmond, Virginia
Author of *On the Block: Developing a Biblical Picture for Missional Engagement*

SERVICE

HOW DO I GIVE BACK?

MEZ MCCONNELL
SERIES EDITED BY MEZ MCCONNELL

CHRISTIAN
FOCUS

 **9Marks**

Copyright © Mez McConnell 2020

paperback ISBN 978-1-5271-0472-3
epub ISBN 978-1-5271-0545-4
mobi ISBN 978-1-5271-0546-1

10 9 8 7 6 5 4 3 2 1

Published and reprinted in 2020
by
Christian Focus Publications Ltd,
Geanies House, Fearn, Ross-shire,
IV20 1TW, Great Britain.

www.christianfocus.com
Cover and interior design by Rubner Durais

Printed in the USA

CONTENTS

PREFACE

The book you have in your hands is the final one in a set of 10 that have been many years in the making. The aim of this entire series has been to offer a consecutive set of discipleship resources that will walk new believers through the basics of the Christian faith.

This final book is based on the premise of Ephesians 4:11-13. Christ himself gave the apostles, the prophets, the evangelists, the pastors and teachers, to equip his people for works of service, so that the body of Christ may be built up until we all reach unity in the faith and in the knowledge of the Son of God and become mature, attaining to the whole measure of the fullness of Christ. The aim of our entire series has been to grow disciples of Jesus who, in turn, build each other up in the faith and go on to serve the wider church body for the glory of God.

May the Lord bless richly you as you read through, and teach, the lessons outlined in this book.

Mez McConnell
February 2020

SERIES INTRODUCTION

The First Steps series will help equip those from an unchurched background take the first steps in following Jesus. We call this the 'pathway to service' as we believe that every Christian should be equipped to be of service to Christ and His church no matter your background or life experience.

If you are a church leader doing ministry in hard places, use these books as a tool to help grow those who are unfamiliar with the teachings of Jesus into new disciples. These books will equip them to grow in character, knowledge and action.

Or if you yourself are new to the Christian faith, still struggling to make sense of what a Christian is, or what the Bible actually says, then this is an easy to understand guide as you take your first steps as a follower of Jesus.

There are many ways to use these books.

+   They could be used by an individual who simply reads through the content and works through the questions on their own.

+   They could be used in a one-to-one setting, where two people read through the material before they meet and then discuss the questions together.

+   They could be used in a group setting where a leader presents the material as a talk, stopping for group discussion throughout.

Your setting will determine how you best use this resource.

A USER'S KEY:

As you work through the studies you will come across the following symbols …

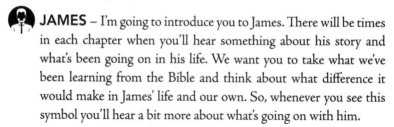

JAMES – I'm going to introduce you to James. There will be times in each chapter when you'll hear something about his story and what's been going on in his life. We want you to take what we've been learning from the Bible and think about what difference it would make in James' life and our own. So, whenever you see this symbol you'll hear a bit more about what's going on with him.

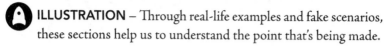

ILLUSTRATION – Through real-life examples and fake scenarios, these sections help us to understand the point that's being made.

STOP – When we hit an important or hard point we'll ask you to stop and spend some time thinking or chatting through what we've just learnt. This might be answering some questions, or it might be hearing more of James' story.

KEY VERSE – The Bible is God's Word to us, and therefore it is the final word to us on everything we are to believe and how we are to behave. Therefore we want to read the Bible first, and we want to read it carefully. So whenever you see this symbol you are to read or listen to the Bible passage three times. If the person you're reading the Bible with feels comfortable, get them to read it at least once.

MEMORY VERSE – At the end of each chapter we'll suggest a Bible verse for memorisation. We have found Bible memorisation to be really effective in our context. The verse (or verses) will be directly related to what we've covered in the chapter.

SUMMARY – Also, at the end of each chapter we've included a short summary of the content of that chapter. If you're working your way through the book with another person, this might be useful to revisit when picking up from a previous week.

INTRODUCTION

We've been asking the big questions in these books. Who are we? Who's God? Is God real? We've thought about whether the Bible can be trusted, and whether Jesus is the Saviour He says He is. If the Bible can be trusted, if God is real, if Jesus is the Saviour (and we all know that we need to be saved), then we've found our answers to life's biggest questions.

So now, if you trust Jesus, the Holy Spirit has shown you that He is the King and you're setting out to live for Him. You want to listen to His word; you want to do what He says and tell others about the hope you've found in Him. Things might be looking rosy – you're living for Jesus! Enjoying His people, the church! You've been forgiven! You've been changed!

And then you run straight into the Christian call to serve others. It's clear in the Bible – we are blessed by God so that we will be a blessing to others. The nitty-gritty of that service, though, isn't easy. It can be tedious, and it's often downright annoying, frustrating and discouraging. When we try to serve others, we face our own sin and theirs. We face the lies which tell us we can't do it, we're not worth anything, we've got nothing to offer.

But the truth of the gospel changes all that. Now our hope is not in what *we* can do, but in the work of Christ in us.

In this book we'll ask more questions, and practical ones. Now that we trust Jesus, now that He's our King – how do we get on and follow Him day by day?

Is anyone just too far gone to help others? Why do we have to serve, anyway? What about my time, my stuff, my money – do I have to give it all away? How can I give if I don't have enough for myself and my family? *Who* am I supposed to serve? What if I just don't want to do it? What will motivate me? What's all this about 'spiritual gifts' – have *I* got any? If so, how am I supposed to use them?

You can read this book alone or with friends, but read it with a willingness to learn more about Jesus and your place as a servant in His beloved body, the Church.

MEET JAMES

James is a new Christian from a working-class background. He grew up on a tough council estate in the Midlands, England. He has battled alcoholism on and off for many years but has remained sober since his conversion twelve months ago.

James is in his mid-thirties, single and has never held down a steady job. He hangs around the church building most of the week and often complains of being bored. He claims he is too ill to work and is worried that even a part-time job would affect his government benefits. He has agreed to study the Bible with you on the subject of Christian service.

WHAT'S THE POINT?
It's not about me, it's about God and His Glory.

1. CAN GOD USE SOMEONE LIKE ME?

GOD USED WHO?!

Can you imagine a prostitute being used by God? What about a lonely widow grieving the loss of her husband and both sons? Or a pregnant, unwed teenager? How could these women possibly be of use to the Lord?

How about a coward being used in one of the most dramatic rescues ever? Or a young shepherd boy bringing down Israel's fiercest enemy? What about a man who sent another woman's husband to his death so he could have his wife? Or a testosterone-driven man who couldn't resist the temptations of a beautiful woman?

Believe it or not, these are all true stories in the Bible.

> God used Rahab the prostitute to help His spies escape from Jericho when they were scoping out the Promised Land (Josh. 2).

> God used Naomi to bring about the marriage of Ruth and Boaz, which eventually led to the birth of Jesus (Ruth 3–4).

> God used young Mary to conceive and give birth to the Son of God, Jesus (Luke 1:26-38).

> God used fearful, stammering Moses to rescue God's people from slavery in Egypt (Exod. 4).

God used young David and his slingshot to bring down Goliath with just a single stone (1 Sam. 17).

God used David as king to lead the nation of Israel, even calling him 'a man after God's own heart' – despite David getting Bathsheba pregnant and then murdering her husband, Uriah, to cover it up (2 Sam. 11).

God used Samson, after his foolish pursuit of multiple women and love-induced confession to Delilah, to dramatically execute judgment on the Philistines in the moment of his own death (Judg. 14–16).

The Bible is full of weak, sinful people failing to do what is right again and again.

JAMES

Why? Why is the Bible full of failures, misfits and criminals? Isn't the Bible meant to show us how we should live, how to do the right thing?

STOP

What do we think of James' question? Is he right or is he wrong?

Is one of the reasons God gave us these stories so that we can feel better about ourselves? I mean when we measure ourselves up to this group of losers, It's easy to think that at least we're not as bad as them! Or is God showing us these failures as a warning to us? Maybe this is God's way of saying to us, 'Watch out, or this could happen to you.'

I don't think either of those thoughts are correct. The Bible hasn't been written to make us feel better, and nor is it a warning that what happened to people back then could happen to us today. That's not to say that there are no consequences for our sins.

There quite clearly are. But, I think we read these stories in our Bibles because they are meant to push us toward Jesus. They are meant to help us to realise that:

WE NEED A HERO

Here's the point: The Bible is not mainly about the people in it. And the Bible isn't mainly about you or me. Yes, the Bible has 'do's and don'ts' in it, but it is not primarily a set of rules.

The Bible is about God. God is the hero, the main character, the main act and the star turn!

 ILLUSTRATION

There's nothing like a rousing battle scene. Think *Lord of the Rings* – the good guys advance, struggle, only to advance again. We love it even more when the underdog rallies to defeat a larger-than-life bully. But in God's story, the only one winning any victory is God. One story about a fear-filled bloke named Gideon shows us how much God cares about His own glory. God deliberately shaves down the army of the Israelites from about 32,000 to only 300 men, just so they won't think that they were the ones who won the battle:

 'The LORD said to Gideon, "The people with you are too many for me to give the Midianites into their hand, lest Israel boast over me, saying, 'My own hand has saved me.' Now therefore proclaim in the ears of the people, saying, 'Whoever is fearful and trembling, let him return home and hurry away from Mount Gilead.'" Then 22,000 of the people returned, and 10,000 remained.

And the LORD said to Gideon, "The people are still too many. Take them down to the water, and I will test them for you there, and anyone of whom I say to you, 'This one shall go with you,' shall go with you, and anyone of whom I say to you, 'This one shall not go with you,' shall not go." … So the people took provisions in their hands, and their

trumpets. And he sent all the rest of Israel every man to his tent, but retained the 300 men. And the camp of Midian was below him in the valley.

…And he divided the 300 men into three companies…

…So Gideon and the hundred men who were with him came to the outskirts of the camp at the beginning of the middle watch, when they had just set the watch. And they blew the trumpets and smashed the jars that were in their hands. Then the three companies blew the trumpets and broke the jars. They held in their left hands the torches, and in their right hands the trumpets to blow. And they cried out, "A sword for the Lord *and for Gideon!" Every man stood in his place around the camp, and all the army ran. They cried out and fled.'* (Judg. 7:2-4, 8, 16, 19-21)

JAMES

I still don't see how God can use someone like me. I have no skills or experience or background. If I had some qualifications, had done an apprenticeship or been a Christian for a long time, maybe I could serve others by teaching the Bible – but what do I have to offer?

STOP

How do you think we should advise James based on what we have learned so far?

The problem is that we tend to look at ourselves first. But remember, God is the hero of this story, not us.

If we get it right, it's only because of God's kindness to us.

When we fail, we are still safe in God's family because of what Jesus did. We have done nothing to earn our salvation. God isn't impressed with our talents, achievements or qualifications. And neither is He put off by our failures, mess-ups and inadequacies. So why do we think we can obey God in our own strength, or please Him out of our own skill?

When we look at ourselves instead of God, we can't see how God will use us. And to be honest, we are right to wonder about that, aren't we? We know our own fears and weaknesses. In the cold light of day, we all know that we make pretty rubbish heroes.

The great news is that God can and does use weak people to do what He wants them to do.

In fact, He specialises in it!

They, and we, do nothing to contribute to God's work. Remember Gideon's sparse army of 300 soldiers – all they did was blow their trumpets and shout, and the enemy went running away!

It is not the strength of the people, or their capacity to serve that makes it happen – it's God alone.

God is the Hero.

God is always the Hero.

Don't get me wrong, it's not that we're irrelevant. God uses individual people, with our own individual strengths, preferences and quirks. **But God gets all of the glory.**

GLORY ADDICTS

One barrier to serving is that we want glory for ourselves. We want to be seen and acknowledged. We want others to admire us. We want people to see how much we've changed, how much we love God, how sacrificial and generous we are. And we don't want to disappoint! So, we're tempted to do two things: we either serve so we look good, or we don't step up and serve in case we mess up.

Better to do nothing and stay cool, than do something and look a complete idiot!

Or maybe we're too busy trying to find glory elsewhere. We look for satisfaction and joy by running after other stuff: relationships, status, gadgets, clothes, television, working out, being fit, having street cred, being valued at work, being clever, being pretty, drugs, sex, pornography, alcohol…the list is endless. We think we know what 'the good life' looks like, and we try to secure it for ourselves. We want to be Somebody: Somebody important. Somebody cool. Somebody respected.

JESUS' KINGDOM OF NOBODIES

But Jesus makes it crystal clear…His kingdom is for nobodies.

In the time of Jesus' earthly life, there were some groups of people universally understood to be nobodies:

children,

women,

tax collectors,

prostitutes,

Gentiles.

The fascinating thing is that Jesus works through each of these groups and shows that they have a place in His Kingdom.

'And they were bringing children to him that he might touch them, and the disciples rebuked them. But when Jesus saw it, he was indignant and said to them, "Let the children come to me; do not hinder them, for to such belongs the kingdom of God. Truly, I say to you, whoever does not receive the kingdom of God like a child shall not enter it."

And he took them in his arms and blessed them, laying his hands on them.' (Mark 10:13-15)

His kingdom isn't about the cool and the hip, the biggest or the baddest, the brightest or the best. It's about nobodies. And even if you are someone, that will keep you *out* of the kingdom rather than get you into it. But when the nobodies are let in, they're welcomed with an open heart and open arms!

BOAST IN THE LORD

In his first letter to the Corinthian church, Paul shows that all strength and power come from Jesus Christ alone, through the gospel. The believers in Corinth had been bickering about which church leader was best. Paul's letter is like a jug of ice-cold water thrown in your face. He says, 'Come on people, it's not about us! Was Paul crucified for you? Of course not! It's all about Jesus!'

Paul rebukes the believers because they were giving Paul, Cephas and Apollos (the other church leaders) too much credit. Christ is the wisdom and power of God, not them. Paul writes that Christ sent him to *'preach the gospel, and not with words of eloquent wisdom, lest the cross of Christ be emptied of its power'* (1 Cor. 1:17).

Paul goes on to remind these Corinthian Christians of their roots:

'For consider your calling, brothers: not many of you were wise according to worldly standards, not many were powerful, not many were of noble birth. But God chose what is foolish in the world to shame the wise; God chose what is weak in the world to shame the strong; God chose what is low and despised in the world, even things that are not, to bring to nothing things that are, so that no human being might boast in the presence of God. And because of him you are in Christ Jesus, who became to us wisdom from God, righteousness and sanctification and redemption, so that, as it is written, "Let the one who boasts, boast in the Lord."' (1 Cor. 1:26-31)

Jesus is building His radical, upside-down Kingdom of useless, fumbling, weak, incapable, worthless sinners who have been transformed by grace alone. And He's doing that to show how great God is and how unstoppable His power is at work in us! We are those who can boast *only* in the Lord.

The only thing that can drive our service, and keep it going when the going gets tough, is God's glory.

It's not about us!

That's what frees us to serve. It's not about our capacity – it's not about our background: whether we've been morally good all our lives or been to the bottom of the pit and back again. **It's only ever about God and what He can do with and through sinners, for His glory.**

When we ask, 'Can God use someone like me?' the answer is a big, loud 'Yes!'

He can, and He will – for the glory of His own powerful, beautiful, merciful name.

MEMORY VERSE

'For even the Son of Man came not to be served but to serve, and to give his life as a ransom for many.' (Mark 10:45)

SUMMARY

God is the Hero! He will use us for the glory of His great name. We rejoice and boast in Jesus alone!

WHAT'S THE POINT?

Because Jesus served us, we are free to serve Him and others.

2. WHY SHOULD WE SERVE?

RECAP

We've seen that God delights to use weak, sinful failures to do His work, in His strength and for His glory.

We wrongly want that glory for ourselves, but we look to Jesus and see that His Kingdom is for nobodies!

God alone gets the glory for what He does in and through us.

We thank God for His amazing work to save us! We can boast only in Him.

JAMES

James considers himself a happy-go-lucky person, even though he takes anti-depressants. He thinks of himself as a selfless person. 'I'll do anything for anybody!' he says. Although, in the next breath, he says that his main aim in life is to 'look after number one!'

TO SERVE OR BE SERVED

'Joy can only be real if people look upon their life as a service and have a definite object in life outside themselves and their personal happiness.' – Leo Tolstoy

'We need to find the courage to say no to the things and people that are not serving us if we want to rediscover ourselves and live our lives with authenticity.' – Barbara De Angelis

Here we have two different ideas about finding happiness: self-sacrifice or self-care. Which is it?

Is Tolstoy right?

> Are our lives designed for serving others? Can we only have real joy when we look outside of ourselves?

Or is Barbara De Angelis right?

> Is life about figuring out what serves us, and getting rid of all the rest?

Apart from the mercy of God, we will all default to the second opinion. If we're not serving God, then we're serving ourselves and expecting everyone else to serve us, too.

YOU GOTTA SERVE SOMEBODY

Bob Dylan – the brilliant songwriter and folk singer – captured this truth about humanity in one song. The chorus says, 'It may be the devil, or it may be the Lord but you're gonna have to serve somebody.'[1] If you haven't heard the song, stop right now and go listen to it. Aside from being deeply theological, it is a rock and roll classic.

This chapter asks: 'Why should we serve?' But that's a bit of a trick question. We don't really have a choice. The most independent, free-spirited, law-ignoring, butt-kicking anarchist is bound fast by this law of humanity: *we all serve somebody.*

---

1   Bob Dylan, 'Gotta Serve Somebody,' *Slow Train Coming*, Columbia Records, 1979.

The only question really is *who* is it going to be?

We will either serve God and others, or we'll serve ourselves. **Without the saving work of Jesus for us and in us, we will always default to self-worship.** We simply cannot serve others unless our hearts are radically re-created to worship and gladly serve our Maker.

JAMES

But that can't be true! What about all those who aren't Christians but do good and serve others? Sometimes non-Christians are more loving and kind than Christians!

STOP

What do we think about what James says here?

There are two points to consider: first, *God cares about our hearts.* It's possible to look like we're doing stuff for others when we're really out to serve ourselves. Second: *God graciously allows all creation to reflect His kindness.* God even allows people who couldn't care less about Him to reveal something of His own goodness, whether they acknowledge Him or not. This is called common grace.

DO-GOODERS AND SELF-SERVERS

God makes it clear that our behaviour, though significant, is far less important than what's going on inside:

'For the LORD sees not as man sees: man looks on the outward appearance, but the Lord looks on the heart.' (1 Sam. 16:7)

This is bad news for us because we humans are excellent at making ourselves look good to others. We do this in ways that are obviously wrong, like telling a lie to save face or gossiping about someone to look like we're better than they are. But we also like to take good things and use them to our advantage: helping a neighbour worse off than ourselves; volunteering at the local homeless shelter to show how concerned we are about others; covering a shift at work to get some cred with the boss. The truth is that any generous, thoughtful or good thing we do can (and usually does) involve some less-than-admirable motivation. We talked about this in the last chapter – it is the same desire to grab glory for ourselves.

Jesus directed some of His strongest 'tell-it-as-it-is' language towards the Pharisees. They did good to look good, but refused to honour God in their hearts:

'Woe to you, scribes and Pharisees, hypocrites! For you are like whitewashed tombs, which outwardly appear beautiful, but within are full of dead people's bones and all uncleanness. So you also outwardly appear righteous to others, but within you are full of hypocrisy and lawlessness.' (Matt. 23:27-28)

We, too, can appear outwardly righteous to others while we are full of 'all uncleanness' within. We can appear to be serving others when we are really serving our own idea of how to be a good person. In this we're making ourselves look or feel good, and we're really serving – worshipping – ourselves.

Or – and this might be more common in our culture today – we take it as a given that we *should* actively pursue our own desires. People, things, circumstances should be serving *us*, or we boot them out. In fact, we owe it to ourselves to get rid of them like some sort of excess baggage. Again, we're serving or worshipping ourselves.

Selfishness is at the bottom of every action, good or bad, from a heart that is not given to Jesus. But serving ourselves (surely the definition of selfishness) is slavery. Sin is a cruel taskmaster – always promising, never delivering.

This condition plagues all humanity, and can only be fixed by a radical re-making of our rotting, self-centred hearts.

IT IS FINISHED!

The good news is that this is exactly what Jesus accomplished on the Cross. God promised to give His people new, softened hearts that are alive to serve the one true God – and that is just what He did. We are now free to serve the one we were made to serve. We are free to worship the one who deserves our worship. We are free to enjoy a real relationship with our Creator, knowing that our sins are covered and our future is secure. And we are free to know the life and joy of giving our lives away.

JAMES

What? How can we find life and joy by giving our lives away? That's just plain stupid!

STOP

How would we help James understand this?

THE SERVANT KING

'Then the mother of the sons of Zebedee came up to him (Jesus) with her sons, and kneeling before him she asked him for something. And he said to her, "What do you want?" She said to him, "Say that these two sons of mine are to sit, one at your right hand and one at your left, in your kingdom." Jesus answered, "You do not know what you are asking. Are you able to drink the cup that I am to drink?" They said to him, "We are able." He said to them, "You will drink my cup, but to sit at my right hand and at my left is not mine to grant, but it is for those for whom it has been prepared by my Father." And when the

ten heard it, they were indignant at the two brothers. But Jesus called them to him and said, "You know that the rulers of the Gentiles lord it over them, and their great ones exercise authority over them. It shall not be so among you. But whoever would be great among you must be your servant, and whoever would be first among you must be your slave, even as the Son of Man came not to be served but to serve, and to give his life as a ransom for many." (Matt. 20:20-28)

Here we have a story of an ambitious mum, who was also probably Jesus' aunt. She wanted the best for her two sons. Being the sister of Jesus' mother Mary, she likely thought her family relationship would guarantee a kind of status. So she stepped right up to the King and asked Him to secure a place of high position in His Kingdom for her boys. But what did Jesus say?

Being wise and kind, He did not tell His aunty off for her cheeky request. He said to her, and her sons who shared her ambition to be top dog, 'You do not know what you are asking.'

When He spoke about drinking the cup, Jesus wasn't talking about a glass of wine. When a military general won a great victory, he would drink a goblet of wine in celebration and be toasted for his victory. But Jesus was not talking about a glorious victory over Israel's enemies, nor about a Jewish nation set free from the oppressive Roman army.

Jesus wasn't that kind of king.

No, *this* cup is the cup of God's judgment, which Jesus fully drank to pay for the sins of His people.[2] Jesus is talking about the agony He will endure at Calvary, when the full force of the Father's righteous anger against sin comes smashing down on His holy

---

2   Matthew 26:39.

head. One song lyric describes the crucifixion this way: 'In three hours Christ suffered more than any sinner ever will in hell.'[3]

But the disciples don't understand what Jesus is really saying. Yet.

Jesus isn't only trying to give them a heads-up about His coming death. He's also a king bringing in a kingdom, but He's a new kind of king ruling over a new kind of kingdom:

a kingdom of servants, ruled by a Servant King.

The disciples must have had a 'what's He talking about?' moment when Jesus told them that, in His kingdom, those who would be great must be servants and those who would be first must be slaves. They were expecting Jesus to defeat their enemies and reign in power on an earthly throne then and there.

They were expecting glory now.

Of course, they hadn't yet seen Jesus the Messiah's torturous death. Jesus came *'not to be served, but to serve, and to give his life as a ransom for many.'* Jesus Himself is the ultimate servant. We serve because He first served us. Jesus did not consider

His own status,

His own preferences,

the injustice of taking punishment for the sins of others,

the agony of absorbing the Father's wrath when He deserved only the Father's pleasure and delight.

Jesus willingly gave His life.

---

3   Shai Linne, 'The Cross (3 Hours)', *The Atonement*, Lamp Mode Recordings, 2008.

Our good news hinges on a suffering, self-sacrificing, servant-hearted King.

THE RISEN KING

But the story doesn't end with the grave. We have life because Jesus died a criminal's death for us, and then He walked physically out of the tomb.

This – the gospel – is our final motivation. Jesus is alive! Because He is alive, we will also live again. Our Servant King accomplished His work, rose from the grave and is even now reigning in glory. All of history is unfolding according to His plan. We have been saved, ransomed, snatched back from the jaws of death and the grip of Satan, to live in purity and joy as God's forever people.

Our Saviour lives! And because He lives, we live to serve Him.

Remember those sons of Zebedee, angling for top seats in Jesus' kingdom? Jesus told them, 'You will drink my cup' — and indeed they did. They followed Jesus in suffering. The two brothers were James and John. James became the first of the apostles to be martyred, killed 'with the sword' by 'violent hands.'[4] John suffered under intense persecution and exile on the island of Patmos.[5]

Truly, James and John served their King and they served His church. And they are now alive with Jesus in glory. This is the hope we have in Christ!

We *should* serve, yes. Absolutely. We are commanded countless times in the Bible to serve others, to consider others first, to love, to give, to work for others. Serving our God and serving others is not optional. It really is a command.

---

4   Acts 12:2.

5   Revelation 1:9.

But the joy of it is that as we think long and deep about our risen, Servant King, as the Holy Spirit works in our hearts, we *want* to serve. And when the going gets tough, we *want* to want to serve! This is God's good work in us.

MEMORY VERSE

'Serve wholeheartedly, as if you were serving the Lord, not people.' (Eph. 6:7, NIV)

SUMMARY

'Why should we serve?' isn't quite the right question, because we all serve somebody. Apart from God's grace, that somebody will be ourselves. With God's grace, though, we are remade into new creatures who are free from the slavery of self-service. We are free to serve God and others. We now find life and joy in giving our lives away.

WHAT'S THE POINT?

Everything we have is from God and belongs to God.

3. STEWARDSHIP (IT'S MY LIFE?)

RECAP

We've seen that God is the Hero – He delights to use weakness to show His strength, and His is an upside-down Kingdom where the nobodies (all of us) are somebody in Him and can serve with joy. We've also seen that we are compelled to serve because we have been gloriously served by our King Jesus. We love because He first loved us; we serve because He first served us.

This chapter is about stewardship, so let's define the term. The *English Oxford Living Dictionary* defines it as: '*The job of supervising or taking care of something, such as an organization or property.*'

Understood biblically, stewardship is God's command for humans to take care of what God gives them. We see it at the very beginning of the Bible story. God has just created the whole beautiful world, including man and woman, and He gives them the responsibility to care for the rest of creation:

'*And God blessed them. And God said to them, "Be fruitful and multiply and fill the earth and subdue it, and have dominion over the fish of the sea and over the birds of the heavens and over every living thing that moves on the earth."*' (Gen. 1:28)

Do you think Adam and Eve thought that this perfect new world belonged to them? If so, why? If not, why not?

It's a bit of both, really. Adam and Eve would have had to be rather thick to imagine that the world belonged to them in the sense that they somehow owned it. Creation was designed and crafted by someone who wasn't them. It was given to them as a gift. They were part of the creation, not the cause of it! So, in one sense, of course it wasn't *their* world.

But on the other hand, Adam and Eve were given authority to take care of this world – to work the land, to care for the animals, to eat of the vegetation. They were the overseers and caretakers of God's good creation. Their authority was real, and so was their responsibility. When Eve carried their first baby, she would have had a deep sense of responsibility, and even ownership, for her offspring. And when Adam followed Eve in disobeying God and so sending the whole of creation plunging into judgment, we are shown the weight of his responsibility as our representative.

Stewardship is important – its authority and responsibility are real.

In effect, stewardship is being called to look after what belongs to God. The danger we face is believing that *we* have ownership – that it all really belongs to us and so we can do with it what we please.

IT'S MY LIFE?

Bon Jovi's hit song of 2000, 'It's My Life', sums up the basic philosophy of our time:

'It's my life
It's now or never

I ain't gonna live forever
I just want to live while I'm alive
(It's my life)
My heart is like an open highway
Like Frankie said
I did it my way
I just want to live while I'm alive
It's my life[1]

The song wasn't a hit just because it was a catchy dance-floor anthem. The bold lyrics appeal to a culture that values personal freedom.

We are part of this culture. As we think about serving others, we start with an illusion about ourselves and our stuff: that it's 'my' life and 'my' stuff. Our sense of ownership comes naturally, doesn't it? Take one peek into a group of small children playing and you're bound to hear 'that's MINE!' – 'no, MINE!' Of course, the fight is ridiculous because the toddlers have done absolutely nothing to get those toys. They are entirely dependent on the adults in their lives to provide for their needs and desires.

We might be too grown-up to hit little Mark over the head with the truck he snatched, but in our hearts we find the very same protest:

'That pay packet is mine, so I can do what I like with it.'

'This home is mine, and I need it to be a place of escape from the stress of life.'

'My time is my own, and I have every right to use it as I want.'

---

1   Bon Jovi, 'It's My Life', *Crush*, Island Records, 2000.

We forget that God is our Father, who gives us all that we have. We are alive moment by moment only because He is sustaining us. We keep on breathing because God keeps our hearts pumping.

Think of the last time your plans got interrupted. I bet that your response revealed how much you believe that your time is your own. I can safely make this bet because I do the same thing!

Despite all we know about God being the Hero and Jesus rescuing us into a life we could never earn, we still labour under the delusion that we have the right to run our own lives apart from our Father's control.

We continue to act as if the stuff we have is due to us.

We treat our time and our plans as our own, to be used as we see fit.

Essentially, we want to be the kings of our own kingdoms.

STOP

What are you particularly tempted to think of as exclusively yours? Time? Money? Health? Spouse/boyfriend/girlfriend? Children? Job? Recreation? Fitness? Possessions?

IT'S GOD'S LIFE

Of course, the truth Christians have come to know is that we have life *only in and through Christ*. Bon Jovi got quite a few things wrong in that song, but perhaps the deadliest lie is this: 'It's now or never; I ain't gonna live forever.'

The truth about humanity is that we are going to live forever – the question is, where? Where will we spend eternity? When we trust

Jesus' work on the cross and His resurrection we can look forward to eternity in glory!

But as the Christian rapper Shai Linne articulated: '*If you're living your best life now you're headed for hell.*'[2] Our tight grip on God's gifts is dangerously short-sighted.

It is because this life is *not* our only life,

> because we *are* going to live forever,

> because it is *not* now or never

> that we can live as the stewards we are meant to be.

First, we see that everything and every relationship we have is a gift from our good Father. So, our job is to look after our Father's people and our Father's stuff. It's not ours; it's His.

Second, we know that we have a much better future ahead of us than any dream lifestyle we could conjure up in the here and now. We don't need to grasp after all that our heart desires in this life – our best life is yet to come!

Again, Jesus is our example. Can you imagine Jesus singing 'It's My Life'? Yet, Jesus is the only one who could ever have any right to sing this song – '*For by him all things were created, in heaven and on earth, visible and invisible, whether thrones or dominions or rulers or authorities — all things were created through him and for him*'[3] – yet our Saviour said to His Father, '*not my will, but yours, be done.*'[4]

And we are called to the same kind of humility:

---

2   Shai Linne, 'Fal$e Teacher$', *Lyrical Theology, Part 1: Theology*, 2013 Lamp Mode Recordings.

3   Colossians 1:16.

4   Luke 22:42.

'Have this mind among yourselves, which is yours in Christ Jesus, who, though he was in the form of God, did not count equality with God a thing to be grasped, but emptied himself, by taking the form of a servant, being born in the likeness of men. And being found in human form, he humbled himself by becoming obedient to the point of death, even death on a cross.' (Phil. 2:5-8)

Jesus Himself gave up His fair claim to power. As His followers with no such claim, we are called to do the same. This changed outlook on life frees us to truly serve the King who bought us. When we know who our King is and who we are in Him, we know that nothing we have is our own. Jesus is the King – we owe Him everything!

WHAT A KING; WHAT A KINGDOM!

Look at Mark 10:29-31:

'Jesus said, "Truly, I say to you, there is no one who has left house or brothers or sisters or mother or father or children or lands, for my sake and for the gospel, who will not receive a hundredfold now in this time, houses and brothers and sisters and mothers and children and lands, with persecutions, and in the age to come eternal life. But many who are first will be last, and the last first."'

Can you see what Jesus is saying?

He's saying that giving up your claim on *everything* you have (possessions, family, relationships, desires, status, ambitions, reputation, popular opinion…life itself!) is part and parcel of what it means to follow Him.

Jesus is also saying that despite these so-called worldly losses, you actually gain all that really matters. Because in Jesus' kingdom, no one is lonely, hungry, destitute, abandoned, homeless or isolated.

In the world over which Jesus rules, singles have families and families have open homes.

No one is left out or forgotten.

This is life under the good reign of a kind King! This is the community of love that Jesus came to create.

This is the community that grows up out of the soil of soft-hearted followers of the King, offering back His gifts, for His glory.

OUR RANSOMED LIVES

Of course, there is a cost to following Jesus. It costs everything we've got. But let's never forget that everything is His in the first place.

There's a Christian song with the lyric: 'Oh Father, use my ransomed life in any way You choose.'[5] I always have a sense of foreboding when singing that song because I know the struggle in my heart to believe it. It's the right prayer, but do I really want to pray it? Do I really want God to 'take me up on it'?

I know people, for example, who have said 'no' to romantic relationships because of their love for Christ and commitment to His cause. They have walked away from a potential husband or wife because they couldn't have Jesus and that person. I know there will be times when they question that decision. But Jesus says to them that they have gained far more than they have lost.

The problem is often that, when we hear those stories, our hearts suddenly harden in fear and self-preservation.

But hard hearts just don't cut it in the kingdom.

---

5   Sovereign Grace Music, 'All I Have is Christ,' *Together for the Gospel Live II*, 2012.

Hard hearts turn you in on yourself.

They fill you with self-pity.

Hard hearts make sure the front door stays closed.

Hard hearts keep **my** marriage, **my** family, **my** singleness, **my** home and **my** possessions all about **me** and **mine**.

This is what the Bible describes as idolatry. Idols have very little to do with statues carved out of wood. They are anything in which we invest our hopes, our dreams and our purpose. They are God-substitutes. It's important to recognise that even good things become bad things when they become god things. And good things make the worst kind of idol because they are so easy to rationalise and justify.

For example, when our love for a person or thing grows so intense that we cannot live without him/her/it, our love then becomes warped and idolatrous. We grip what is 'ours' so tightly that our hearts grow hardened. Two things then happen:

1. The thing we're holding so tightly to proves itself incapable of carrying the load we're placing on it, and

2. That very thing begins to own, control and crush us.

The good news is that Jesus died to rescue us from such servitude and bondage.

There is a beautiful paradox in the principle of stewardship: we must let go of our grip to properly take care of what God gives.

Only hearts won by Christ and for Christ beat for the good of others. This is the beauty of the kingdom – the beauty of the

King. *It costs everything we've got and we gain more than we could ever imagine.*

So, how will we take care of God's things, and His people for His glory?

MEMORY VERSE

'I appeal to you therefore, brothers, by the mercies of God, to present your bodies as a living sacrifice, holy and acceptable to God, which is your spiritual worship.' (Rom. 12:1)

SUMMARY

As stewards, we are called to be responsible for and look after what belongs to God. But we easily begin to believe that it all really belongs to us. Remembering that all we have is from our kind Father motivates us to give and serve freely. After all, it's His stuff, not ours! And as we give up 'our' lives in service to God and others, we gain the immeasurable blessings of obedience. All that is good in our lives is a gift of extravagant kindness and generosity.

WHAT'S THE POINT?

As served sinners, we serve sinners.

4. WHO SHOULD WE SERVE?

RECAP

So far, we've talked about
(1) who God can use,
(2) why we should serve, and
(3) stewardship.

I hope that two main ideas have stuck with you: first, God is the Hero of this story – it really is all about Him and His glory! And second, this Hero humbled Himself to death on a cross to seek and save the lost. Our powerful, big God is the ultimate servant. This alone motivates us to obey His command to serve others and be good stewards of His gifts to us.

WHO SHOULD WE SERVE?

It's quite a list, and probably helpful to get it out there at the beginning. There's no small print when it comes to being part of God's kingdom! As those who have been liberated by Christ from sin, self and Satan, we are set free to serve:

+ God

+ Other Christians

+ Those we like

+ Those we don't like

+ Those who aren't like us

+ Even those who don't like us

In short, we serve anyone and everyone. Martin Luther, the German monk who kicked off the Reformation around 500 years ago, put it this way: **'A Christian is a perfectly free lord of all, subject to none. A Christian is a perfectly dutiful servant of all, subject to all.'**[1]

But which is it? Either a Christian is under no one's authority, or a Christian is under the authority of all people and a servant of others. It can't be both, surely!?

JAMES

How does that work? How can a Christian be both 'perfectly free' and 'a perfectly dutiful servant'? I don't understand.

STOP

How would you help James understand this truth?

Yes. It can and must be both. A Christian is someone 'perfectly free' in the Lord. We follow Christ alone: we have been won by Him and freed from slavery to sin; no other person has power over us. But at the same time, our King calls us to lay down our preferences and pride, submitting to the authority and preferences of others. This is the 'consider others first' principle.

Luther described a key aspect of living as a follower of Jesus: our King asks us to lay down our lives in service of others, while our entire allegiance belongs to Him alone.

So, we don't serve like slaves who have no choice. We can joyfully serve others only *because* we have been served by our one true Servant King.

But our question is about *who* we should serve. Luther says that a Christian is a 'perfectly dutiful servant of *all*, subject to *all*.' Who should we serve? We should serve *all* – everyone!

STOP

Consider all the people you meet in a day: the shop assistant, your children's teacher, your friends, your kids, your fellow drivers on the road, your neighbours. What would it look like for you to serve these people? Give examples. How might you serve the bus driver? How do you serve your family? Your boss? Your friends?

We see that we should serve *all people*…but what is the nitty-gritty of serving others? What does it look like in real life? Unsurprisingly, the Bible is very helpful here.

SERVING IN THE FAMILY

In western culture, the individual is the centre of all things. In contrast, as we have seen in the Bible, God is the centre of all things. But the God of the Bible is one God in three persons: Father, Son and Holy Spirit. He is a relational God, and the truth about who He is as one God in three persons is essential to His identity and nature. This is the God whose image we bear, which explains our desire and capacity for relationships. We reflect God's nature in the way we want and need others, and others are essential to who we are as human beings.

When we become Christians we are not simply saved to enjoy a personal relationship with God; **we are rescued from our individualism and isolationism.** By being brought into a relationship with God we are brought into relationship with others.

But what does it look like to serve this new family into which we have been brought?

The New Testament is full of passages that highlight the essential relational dimension of our identity as Christians. Here are just a handful of examples:

First and foremost, we are to **love one another** (John 13:34). This command to love one another runs all throughout the New Testament. In John's letter, he continuously tells his readers to love one another (1 John 3:11; 4:7, 11; 2 John 5). 1 John 3:23[2] shows just how important this is. It's as important as the command to believe in the name of Jesus! Romans 12:10 says we are to '*love one another with brotherly affection.*' When we serve others, we love them with brotherly or sisterly affection. It's not just a duty, but a joy. We enjoy listening to them. We think about them with warmth. We treat them as family.

Romans 12:10 goes on to say that we should '*outdo one another in showing honour.*' So we are to **honour one another.** We show honour to others by considering them first, by viewing them as important and valuable. But that doesn't always come easily, does it? Pride is often a bigger problem than we care to admit, and thinking of ourselves more highly than we should will always lead to a critical and judgmental attitude toward others.

If we are going to refuse to sit in judgment on one another, we will need to learn how to **welcome one another** ('*welcome one another as Christ has welcomed you, for the glory of God*' [Rom. 15:7]). Once we recognise who we are in the gospel, and begin to appreciate what God has done for us in Christ, the exhortation in Galatians 5:13[3] is both an encouragement and a possibility.

---

2   1 John 3:23: 'And this is his commandment, that we believe in the name of his Son Jesus Christ and love one another, just as he has commanded us.'

3   Galatians 5:13: 'For you were called to freedom, brothers. Only do not use your freedom as an opportunity for the flesh, but through love serve one another.'

Paul tells us we are called to freedom, but that we are to use that freedom to **serve one another**. We might not want to welcome others for a host of reasons: they dress or speak differently, they're richer or poorer than us, their skin is a different colour than ours, they have different ideas about theology, they find different movies funny, they like hip-hop and we like musicals. We know, from our own experience, that silly things like these can lead us to distance ourselves from others. And that distance makes us not want to serve them. But for God's glory we are called to welcome and accept one another, and then serve one another.

JAMES

But what about the people that I don't like, like my dad? He walked out on us when we were children and he's nothing but a drunken idiot! How am I supposed to serve him?

STOP

With this specific example in mind, who are the people you find it easy to serve? Who might be harder for you to serve? What will you do about it?

KINGDOM SERVING

How and who we serve is radically changed when we become part of God's kingdom. Suddenly we know that we have a new identity. We don't have to suck up to get ahead. And it's even possible for us to mess up and still thrive as a citizen of Christ's kingdom! Our care for others is driven by love for Jesus rather than what we get out of it. And when we are called to serve and love everyone, that's the best possible motivation.

Who do we serve?
+ Those who hate us

There's something wonderfully revolutionary about serving and loving those who hate us.

We all find it much easier to serve our mates. If we're honest, we feel that it's those who like us and who are like us who deserve our care. But the gospel paints a very different picture, doesn't it? We've seen that Jesus served those who did not deserve it. And, in case we forget, that includes you and me! Jesus modelled the subversive glory of serving and loving haters.

He calls us to do good to those who wrong us.

This is an old story, which runs deep through the Bible. Joseph loved and served the brothers who betrayed him. Believers throughout history have served and loved those who sought their harm, painting a striking picture of God's power in the lives of His children.

Let me tell you a story about Dirk Willems, who lived in the sixteenth century. I find this account ridiculous and beautiful, at the same time.

Dirk was running away from an officer of the court. He was a criminal only because he questioned how the State did religion. His crime was being re-baptised as an adult because he didn't think being baptised as a baby was a valid expression of personal belief in Jesus. He was one of a group known as the Anabaptists; they suffered a great deal for their beliefs.

Knowing that his arrest would lead to his death, Dirk managed to escape from prison by making a rope out of bed sheets and climbing down the outside of the building. But he was spotted and pursued. He ran over a frozen lake and managed to make it across, but when the court official tried to follow him the ice broke and the official fell into the freezing water. Dirk could easily have made his escape. But instead, he turned back to rescue the man who, when joined by his officers, promptly arrested Dirk. Willems was subsequently tried and executed. His death by fire is recorded as being long and miserable.[4]

Isn't that a stunning example of what it means to serve our enemies? It seems too good to be true—or too stupid to be real! How you view it will be an indicator of how much your heart has been won by Christ. His rescue of us makes Dirk's sacrifice seem lame by comparison.

Who do we serve?
+ The weak and vulnerable

As I read the Gospel of Luke, I'm drawn to how often we find Jesus hanging out with the rejects of society. He chose to be with them rather than with the rich and powerful. In fact, this was so much the case that He was even described as a drunk and a glutton because He spent that much time hanging out with riff-raff.

These people were abandoned by society. They didn't have the safety net of social security. They had to make it by relying on their own wit and wisdom. Prostitutes, for example, only 'chose' that profession because they had been abandoned by their husbands. Their opportunities were few and their prospects weren't bright. It was the same with the sick and the outcasts. In fact, Jesus went out of His way to reach and serve the rejected and ignored of society. Jesus met them at their point of need and vulnerability.

Who do we serve?
+ The lost

We are all Christians because someone has served us by bringing the gospel to us. At its simplest, we were lost and someone found

---

4   Thieleman J. van Bragt, 'The Martyrs' Mirror', *Herald Press*, 1938, p. 741.

us. Ultimately, that someone is Jesus. But almost always, Jesus uses others to go and find us. As those who were lost but are now found, our hearts long to see others rescued too.

Christians are often accused of being 'holier than thou.' Sadly, we may come across that attitude far too often. But the fact is that Christians are just like everyone else, apart from the fact that we've been rescued by Jesus. We have nothing to be superior about and everything to be thankful for. Being lost is not an achievement to boast in, and being rescued is not a cause for congratulations – as though we did it. If we understand salvation rightly, our hearts will be soft to those who are just like us. And soft hearts result in sacrificial service.

TRUE GREATNESS IN THE KINGDOM

'And they came to Capernaum. And when [Jesus] was in the house he asked them, "What were you discussing on the way?" But they kept silent, for on the way they had argued with one another about who was the greatest. And he sat down and called the twelve. And he said to them, "If anyone would be first, he must be last of all and servant of all." And he took a child and put him in the midst of them, and taking him in his arms, he said to them, "Whoever receives one such child in my name receives me, and whoever receives me, receives not me but him who sent me."' (Mark 9:33-37)

True greatness is measured not by the size of our ego, nor by the 'coolness' of the people who hang out at our place. True greatness is demonstrated in our willingness to be a servant to everyone: the irrelevant, the inconsequential, the nobodies, the anonymous, the stranger, the drop-out, the different. People who not only *don't* enhance our reputation, but may positively ruin it!

Because it's people like that who make up the kingdom over which Jesus rules.

Essentially, none of us deserve it. We serve sinners because as sinners we've been served by a great Saviour. Of course, it's hard. But the cross was no picnic either. And if Christ was willing to endure that for our sakes, then how can we *not* be willing to spill blood, sweat and tears in serving others?

MEMORY VERSE

'*Do not neglect to show hospitality to strangers, for thereby some have entertained angels unawares.*' (Heb. 13:2)

SUMMARY

Who do we serve? Because we have been served, we are free to serve *all* people with genuine care for their well-being. We are called to serve our brothers and sisters in the Lord, of course. But we're also called to serve the vulnerable, the lost, those who hate us, the weak, the poor, the addicted, the rich. We serve regardless of street cred or status, and our love for the weakest and weirdest just shows off the awesome mercy and grace of our Father.

WHAT'S THE POINT?
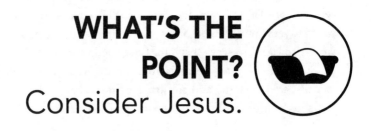
Consider Jesus.

5. WHAT IF I DON'T WANT TO SERVE?

RECAP

In chapter one we talked about the truth that God is the Hero – He delights to use weak people for His glory. Chapter two pointed out that our Servant King, Jesus, is both our reason and power for serving Him and others. In chapter three we came to grips with the reality that all we consider 'ours' is a gift from God! And finally, in chapter four we broke down who we ought to be serving – everyone. But now we'll look at something that gets in the way.

CAN'T BE BOTHERED SYNDROME

By now I hope you've seen that, for a Christian, service is essential. Serving others is not an optional extra to following Jesus. Instead, being a servant is *who we are* in Christ. Jesus served us, so we serve others. It really is that simple.

JAMES

Well, I'm not as selfless as I thought I was. In fact, I am a bit of a selfish rat!

STOP

Think honestly about your behaviour. Does serving God and others feature prominently in your life? Do you think others would describe you as 'willing to serve'?

If you're anything like me, you'll feel the difference between reading about serving and putting it into practice. We have lots of big ideas, don't we?

I'll help with the washing up, for sure.

> But when the time comes, if I'm having a good chat with my mate I'll let others get on with it.

Of course, I'll be there when my friends need someone.

> But when I hear the doorbell ring at 11p.m., I roll over and pull the duvet over my head.

You bet I'll help at church!

> But when the help involves snack time and three-year-olds, I decide that now is not the best time to volunteer.

There is a deep and profound diagnosis for these symptoms, and it has the technical name 'Can't Be Bothered Syndrome.'

Our reluctance to serve is not complicated. It's simply laziness. It's a bit like exercise: we know it's good for us and we have every intention of doing it. But like a diet, it always starts tomorrow!

Now exercise isn't a perfect illustration. For one, it carries tangible results: our endorphin levels increase, making us feel that glow of accomplishment and well-being. Our blood pressure lowers, our heart gets healthier, our muscles get stronger, and our bodies get leaner. But serving others? That doesn't deliver such obvious benefits. It's often a hard slog – tiring and depleting.

But serving and exercise are similar in that we're tempted to shrug them both off due to laziness. We have other things we'd rather do. This is the central issue. Why?

Because we always do what we want to do.

> **STOP**
>
> *You might be thinking, 'Hang on, what? Lots of people don't get to do what they want.' What do you think the phrase 'We always do what we want to do' means? Is it true?*

Doing what we want to do means that we do what we really, deep down, *want* to do. A cleaner might not want to spend all day scrubbing toilets, but she wants to pay her rent. You may not want to hand over your wallet when a knife is put to your throat, but you want to keep your life more than that £10. Whenever human beings do difficult things, there's always an underlying motivation or 'want.' In other words, there's something stronger than the unpleasantness. Athletes don't want to wake up before dawn in the middle of winter to train, but they do want a place at the next competition, and they definitely want a place on the podium!

Bear with me – this does have something to do with serving others. You see, it's easy to be busy when there's a need, or push snooze when your alarm rings in time for an early morning run. But our behaviour is much more significant than we might think because it shows something about what we want, what we really, really want!

If we want to serve more than we want our own comfort, we will be available.

If we want to grow strong and healthy more than we want our own comfort, we will roll out of bed and lace up our running shoes.

We all know that shrugging off exercise has consequences for our bodies, as well as our emotional and spiritual well-being. But shrugging off our call to serve God and others has eternal consequences – because it's disobedience. *Can't Be Bothered Syndrome* can, in fact, be fatal.

In the book of Hebrews, we see one danger of disobedience: it hardens our hearts. Ultimately, when we don't obey it's simply because we don't *want* to obey.

 'Take care, brothers, lest there be in any of you an evil, unbelieving heart, leading you to fall away from the living God. But exhort one another every day, as long as it is called "today," that none of you may be hardened by the deceitfulness of sin. For we have come to share in Christ, if indeed we hold our original confidence firm to the end. As it is said,

"Today, if you hear his voice,
do not harden your hearts as in the rebellion."

For who were those who heard and yet rebelled? Was it not all those who left Egypt led by Moses? And with whom was he provoked for forty years? Was it not with those who sinned, whose bodies fell in the wilderness? And to whom did he swear that they would not enter his rest, but to those who were disobedient? So we see that they were unable to enter because of unbelief.' (Heb. 3:12-19)

JAMES

But my social worker says I have to look after number one. She says that I have to love myself first and foremost. Is she wrong then?

STOP

Is his social worker wrong? Explain to James why she is or isn't.

So what's going on in the heart when we don't want to serve others?

We often try to make things more complicated than they are because it creates the sense that *we're* complicated, which gives us excuses. But the simple reason we don't want to serve others is because we're preoccupied with serving ourselves. As we said earlier, though made to be lovers of God and others, we have all become lovers of self. And as self-lovers, the needs of others are at best an inconvenience and at worst an unforgivable intrusion. After all, if this is my world and I'm god of it, others better get with the programme and start serving me!

Whatever Whitney Houston may have claimed, loving yourself is not the *'greatest love of all.'*[1] It's the most popular, for sure, but it's not the greatest. It consumes us and shrivels us up so we are but a poor and pathetic expression of who we were meant to be.

And yet, it's at this precise point that we see the strange contradiction of the gospel. Let me explain. By refusing to serve others because we're in awe of ourselves, we're *actually* selling ourselves short. We're losing out. After all, Jesus tells us that by holding on to our lives too tightly we lose them, but by letting them go we gain them.

Heaven is only populated with servants because the King of heaven is Himself the greatest servant of all.

The call of Christ on our lives is to forget ourselves and to run after God and others. That's who we were made to be. Don't settle for anything less because you really are selling yourself short if you do. But that's what Can't Be Bothered *SIN*drome does. You see that, don't you? Sin always sells us short.

If we were intended and designed to love God, then we're never going to be whole unless we do. Likewise, if we were intended and

---

1   Whitney Houston, 'Greatest Love of All', *Whitney Houston*, Arista Records, 1985.

designed to love others so that we seek their good above our own, then we'll never be whole unless we do.

Let's get on living that life now.

Let's get on becoming who God made us to be, and who Jesus saved us to be. In other words, let's get serving. For God and His glory, embrace servanthood as good, beautiful and utterly satisfying.

But to be fair, that's easier said than done. So, what's the remedy?

1. Consider Jesus

This was always going to be the place to start, wasn't it? Consider Him who left the throne room of heaven for the slums of earth. The one who took off a crown of gold to take up a crown of thorns. The King who slipped off His robe of splendour to wear an apron of cloth and wash the feet of His followers. The Saviour who laid His glory to one side so that He could carry a cross on His back.

2. Remember James Brown

It was the Godfather of Soul who offered this advice: 'Get Up Offa That Thing'.[2] They aren't the most profound lyrics in the world, and it's doubtful they would win a prize in a poetry contest. The reason James Brown wanted us to 'get up' was so that we might dance and feel better. But the point is well made nonetheless. Sometimes, you just have to *get up offa that thing*; you just have to get on and serve. No more excuses, no more '*mañana, mañana,*' no more maybe – just get up and get on with it.

3. Consider Jesus Again

But even when we shake ourselves out of our stupor and get on with being the servants God wants us to be, we need to

---

2   James Brown, 'Get Up Offa That Thing', *Get Up Offa That Thing*, Polydor Records, 1976.

continuously consider Jesus. Never lose sight of Him. Never forget Him. Always 'have this mind in you which was also in Christ Jesus, who, being in very nature God, did not consider equality with God something to be grasped, but rather emptied himself, taking on the very form of a servant...he humbled himself...' (Phil. 2:5-7)

Keep taking your heart back to Him. And when you find you've forgotten Him, turn from whatever it is that is preoccupying you, and consider Him afresh.

But we shouldn't be naïve about the situations in which we can sometimes find ourselves. There are realities of life in a broken world which genuinely make it hard to serve others:

+ **Sickness** – The spirit may be willing, but the flesh weak. Sickness and infirmity are real reasons why it can be hard to physically serve.

+ **Lack of resources** – Like the flesh, my bank balance may be diminished, my home unsuitable, my car a wreck. I may really want to serve others, but just don't seem to have the wherewithal to do so.

+ **Suffering** – Circumstances can seem to conspire against us so that we are immersed in our own predicaments and necessarily preoccupied with our own problems.

But the remedy in dealing with these obstacles is the same: consider Jesus.

When your circumstances make it hard to serve, look to Jesus.

When you just can't be bothered, look to Jesus.

Seeing sick and suffering Christians choose to consider Jesus is a wonderful testimony to God's grace. Seeing their joy in serving

Him, in spite of circumstances, points to Jesus. In Christ, we are servants whether it's easy or tough. Look to the Saviour and let your heart be daily refreshed by His astounding grace, so that you will enjoy the fullness of who you were always created to be.

MEMORY VERSE

'Have this mind among yourselves, which is yours in Christ Jesus.' (Phil. 2:5)

SUMMARY

Serving others is not always easy. We struggle with laziness, the desire to serve ourselves, and various hardships in our fallen world. But our remedy is the same: look to Christ, our Servant King and Saviour. Consider Him, the one who laid aside His glory to seek and save the lost. If we follow Him, we are servants, too. So let's live like it! It really is our purpose and delight to serve.

WHAT'S THE POINT?

Only the gospel can get us serving and keep us serving.

6. WHAT'S MY MOTIVATION FOR SERVING?

We've discussed a number of questions so far: can God use someone like me? Why should I serve? Who should I serve? What about 'my life'? What if I don't want to serve? Through it all, we've seen that God is the Hero who deserves and requires our devotion and service. And we've seen that serving Him supplies our deepest joy because it's what we were made for. Now we're asking about our motivation for serving. What will get us serving, and keep us serving?

BRASS TACKS

Here we 'get down to brass tacks,' as it were. Here we discuss the deepest, darkest motivations of our hearts:

What makes us tick?

What *should* make us tick?

What's the difference, and how on earth do we get those two things to match up so that we do what we ought to do, and for the right reasons?

STOP

You'll remember that in chapter two we asked, 'why should I serve?' Do you think our question for this chapter ('What's my motivation for serving?') is different? How so?

WHY VS HOW

When we looked at the question 'why should I serve?' we first recognized that we are hardwired to serve because we are created to worship. The question is always WHO will we serve? As followers of Jesus, the gospel requires our obedience in serving God and others. Serving is essential to being a disciple of Jesus.

'What's my motivation for serving?', though, gets to something slightly different. Yes, motivation is about why we do what we do, but it's also got a hint of the how. Motivation is about what's going on in our hearts. What is it that gets us serving and keeps us serving God and others? In other words, what are our reasons for serving, and are they good ones? How do we serve?

SERVICE – THE WIMPY LIFE?

Just to keep it fresh, here's a reminder from the Bible of what it looks like to serve:

'Remind them to be submissive to rulers and authorities, to be obedient, to be ready for every good work, to speak evil of no one, to avoid quarrelling, to be gentle, and to show perfect courtesy toward all people.' (Titus 3:1-2)

JAMES

What? That sounds stupid! How realistic is this? I don't think I can live like that. What about when people bad-mouth me or my family on Facebook? Am I supposed to just let them?

STOP

What do you think? In light of this verse, how should James react to abuse on Facebook? Or from anybody else for that matter?

What on earth would cause someone to live like this? We all know that this kind of life is completely opposite to what comes naturally. In our world, to be 'top dog' you've got to assert your strength, not submit to others. You've got to call the shots, not obey others. In our world, you've got to be aggressive, not gentle. You use words to get what you want, to tear down the competition! If you 'show perfect courtesy to all people' you'll be walked all over, right? This just sounds kind of wimpy.

Why would anyone try to live this way?

Here's the thing: every command in the Bible is there because God is committed to us becoming more like Jesus – the ultimate and true human. The goal of godliness is for our behaviour to sync ever more with the glorious reality of our done-and-dusted union with Christ. It's no good calling someone who follows these commands wimpy unless we're prepared to call Jesus wimpy. If we're imagining what it looks like to live in a Titus 3:1-2 way, then we must imagine Jesus.

> Jesus, who taught His disciples to turn the other cheek, also turned over the tables of the merchants because they were making His Father's house into a house of trade.

> Jesus, who welcomed sinners into fellowship, also spoke severe words of condemnation to the hypocritical Pharisees.

> Jesus was the ultimate example of humility and sacrificial service.

This is because, as we've already seen, Jesus is the King of a very different Kingdom. In His Kingdom, servants are fearless, the humble are strong, and the gentle are bold. In our messed-up world those things usually don't go together, but men and women of the King stand up for justice even as they bow down to serve others. It's a beautiful picture.

THE RIGHT MOTIVE

Why were these believers told to live and serve others in this radically kind, submissive, obedient and gentle way? Was it because, as members of a new religion, they needed to make a good impression? Or maybe they needed to avoid causing waves so they wouldn't face persecution or martyrdom? Was the advice just to get them by on earth with the least amount of trouble?

Nope.

In the first place, they didn't avoid trouble, persecution or martyrdom. Early Christians (and Christians all over the world today) endure suffering, finding hope in Christ.[1]

But back to Titus 3, here's why they were called to live in humility and gentleness:

'For we ourselves were once foolish, disobedient, led astray, slaves to various passions and pleasures, passing our days in malice and envy, hated by others and hating one another.'

In other words, we don't dare look down on others once we've been saved because we've been exactly where they are now. But here's where everything changes:

*'**But** when the goodness and loving kindness of God our Saviour appeared, he saved us, not because of works done by us in righteousness, but according to his own mercy, by the washing of regeneration and renewal of the Holy Spirit, whom he poured out on us richly through Jesus Christ our Saviour, so that being justified by his grace we might become heirs according to the hope of eternal life.'* (Titus 3:4-7)

Because of the goodness and loving kindness of God our Saviour we have been plucked up out of our cesspool of hatred, envy, selfishness and foolishness. And now, having been given new life (regeneration) and renewal by the Holy Spirit, we have been justified and – hear this – we are now heirs according to the hope of eternal life! Our status has gone from the lowest of the low – we were wretched, miserable slaves of sin and despair – to the highest of the high!

We are children of the one true King with the hope of eternal life in glory.

That's our story. Not because we earned it, but by the Father's grace to us – freely available through Jesus' death and resurrection.

Our best motivation for service is intentionally and vividly remembering the grace we have received. As one Christian writer has said, 'Jesus knows that, unless these proud men humble themselves to receive grace, they will never be able to give grace in the way Jesus has served them. Proud sinners who can't receive grace as a gift from God will not be likely to offer it. **You can't serve other sinners if you don't receive Jesus' service for you.** There is no way you will be up for the task.'[2]

DODGY MOTIVES

There are plenty of dodgy motives for serving. To be on our guard, here are a few of them:

+ People-pleasing – serving so others are pleased with us

+ Self-satisfaction – serving so we feel good about ourselves

+ Wanting to be needed – serving because we want to feel essential

---

2   Paul David Tripp and Timothy S. Lane, *Relationships: A Mess Worth Making*, New Growth Press, 2008, p. 126.

♦ Wanting to be appreciated – serving because we want to feel valued

Ultimately, all of these come down to self-salvation. We're driven to serve because in some way, we're trying to make ourselves right with God instead of believing His Word and trusting His work. But that burden is too big for us. It will crush us and our attempts to serve.

MOTIVATED BY JOY

The 1981 film *Chariots of Fire* tells the story of Scottish Olympic runner Eric Liddell. In the film, Liddell says, 'When I run, I feel God's pleasure.'[3] There's joy in using our gifts for God's glory, and we flourish when we live up to what we are called to be – servants of the triune God.

But that doesn't make it 'all about us.' We want to be who God made us to be so that we will bring Him glory because that's ultimately why we were made. He's the one who gets the applause, not us. And in that, we are supremely satisfied.

ILLUSTRATION

Imagine a football team that's made up of quality players, but never realises its full potential. It's always less than the sum of its parts. On paper, the team could beat anyone. There's so much promise, but it's never realised – until a new manager takes over. Somehow, he gets the players playing for each other and for the team. They start to win, even going on a bit of a run. To everyone's surprise, they end up winning the league.

Now, who do you think will be carried around the stadium on the players' shoulders? And do you think that any one of those players will resent the praise given to the manager? Of course not! They know that without him, they would have continued to be a group of under-achieving prima donnas.

That's how it is with us. When we get to heaven, we won't be slapped on the back and told what a great job we did. But then, it won't even enter our heads that we should be. We'll be too busy applauding Jesus because we'll know that it's all because of Him.

People don't have to see what you're doing for it to count before God. In fact, quite the opposite is true. It really doesn't matter if anyone notices. It can be as simple as smiling at a lonely friend at church, or bringing a packet of biscuits to the man recovering from surgery, or cutting the grass for an elderly neighbour, or popping to the shops for a family that just had a baby. All service glorifies God.

So whether you're serving behind the scenes or on stage – whatever, wherever, whenever it is, let 'But God' be your driving motivation:

 *'And you were dead in the trespasses and sins in which you once walked, following the course of this world, following the prince of the power of the air, the spirit that is now at work in the sons of disobedience – among whom we all once lived in the passions of our flesh, carrying out the desires of the body and the mind, and were by nature children of wrath, like the rest of mankind. **But God,** being rich in mercy, because of the great love with which he loved us, even when we were dead in our trespasses, made us alive together with Christ – by grace you have been saved – and raised us up with him and seated us with him in the heavenly places in Christ Jesus, so that in the coming ages he might show the immeasurable riches of his grace in kindness toward us in Christ Jesus. For by grace you have been saved through faith. And this is not your own doing; it is the gift of God, not a result of works, so that no one may boast. For we are*

his workmanship, created in Christ Jesus for good works, which God prepared beforehand, that we should walk in them.' (Eph. 2:1-10)

MEMORY VERSE

'For by grace you have been saved through faith. And this is not your own doing; it is the gift of God.' (Eph. 2:8)

SUMMARY

Our fundamental motivation for serving must be that we have been served. We have been saved – not because of our works, but according to the mercy of God our Saviour, poured out richly on us through Jesus. Any other motivation will be driven by our desire to save ourselves, and will not sustain us for the hard work of serving God and others. Only the gospel will provide lasting strength, hope, joy and motivation in serving.

WHAT'S THE POINT?

Spiritual gifts are given by the Holy Spirit to every believer, to build up the church.

7. WHAT ARE THE SPIRITUAL GIFTS?

We have thought about:

+ God using the weak because HE is the Hero;

+ Being created to serve;

+ Everything we have being *from* God and *for* God;

+ Our calling to be servants of *all*;

+ Getting over 'Can't Be Bothered SIN-drome';

+ Our motivation to serve.

Now we're going to think about something you may have heard people in your Christian community talking about: the spiritual gifts. What are these mystical-sounding things?

JAMES

James recently visited his friend's Pentecostal church and he has come back full of questions. Why don't our services look like theirs? Why don't we worship God like they worship God? He wants to know what you think of the gifts of the Holy Spirit and if he has any of them.

SAY WHAT?

If you've been hanging around Christians for a while, you will almost certainly have heard people talking about 'spiritual gifts.' You may have heard things like, 'She really has the gift of encouragement!' or 'I'm not sure I'm gifted in that way.' Perhaps you've heard about gifts such as speaking in tongues, healing, prophecy or words of knowledge.

So, what *are* spiritual gifts? Is this some kind of weird hocus pocus? How many of them are there? Are these gifts that we give, or gifts we get? How do we get them?

Right at the start we need to be open about the fact that this – and particularly what it means for us today – is an area of controversy among Christians. So, we will try to keep it simple, and navigate as best we can some choppy waters with a few rocks just underneath the surface!

WHAT ARE SPIRITUAL GIFTS?

Here are a few definitions. As you read, see if you can pick out some things they have in common:

'A spiritual gift is any ability that is empowered by the Holy Spirit and used in any ministry of the church.'[1]

'God equips and empowers people for service within the church, which is the body of Christ.'[2]

---

1   Wayne Grudem, *Systematic Theology: An Introduction to Biblical Doctrine*, InterVarsity Press, 1994, p. 1016.

2   Vern S. Poythress, *What are the Spiritual Gifts?*, P&R Publishing, 2010, p. 5.

'Spiritual gifts are an essential, foundational tool in the sanctification process, in the building up of one another in the knowledge and love of Jesus Christ.'[3]

STOP
What connects each of these definitions?

First, each definition points out that *these gifts are given.* They are a gift **from** God.

That makes sense, doesn't it? Spiritual gifts have nothing to do with an airy-fairy, vague or mysterious 'spirituality'. Yes, of course, spiritual gifts may seem a little hard to get our heads around because we can never fully understand God and how He works. But *spiritual* gifts are such because they are given by the Holy Spirit, the third Person of the Trinity.

Second – and this is the point I really want to press – *all three definitions look at spiritual gifts in the context of the Church,* the body of Christ.

This is essential for our understanding of spiritual gifts: they are not individualistic.

They are not given for me and me alone.

They are not given to increase my status and make me more important. They are not primarily for deepening my own walk with the Lord (though they certainly do that).

Rather, spiritual gifts are *for* the body. My growing delight in Jesus, through gifts given by the Spirit, is for the sake of encouraging and helping my brothers and sisters grow in *their* delight in Jesus.

---

3   Sam Storms, from interview on the Desiring God website: http://desiringgod.org/interviews/spiritual-gifts accessed 18th August, 2017.

BACK IT UP

Let's take a few steps backward to see some of the Spirit's work in the Bible – which, after all, is our final authority for the things we believe and how we behave.

We'll focus on Jesus.

Jesus is God. The Bible is very clear that He, as the Son, is every bit as much God as the Father. He is fully God and fully man. But what is really intriguing is how significant and necessary the Holy Spirit was in His life from the very beginning.

Mary, Jesus' mother, was a virgin when she conceived. We're told that, *'before they* [Mary and her fiancée Joseph] *came together* [i.e. had sexual intercourse], *she was found to be with child from the Holy Spirit.'*[4]

> The Holy Spirit was vital for God the Son to become Jesus of Nazareth.

But the Holy Spirit doesn't then disappear. Some thirty years later, Jesus is about to begin His public ministry, and He goes to the River Jordan to be baptised by His cousin, John.

> **Baptism was a dramatic way of showing that you belonged to the people of God, and it involved being immersed or drenched in water.**

But when Jesus is baptised, something else happens. Look at how Mark describes it for us:

'In those days Jesus came from Nazareth of Galilee and was baptised by John in the Jordan. And when he came up out of the water, immediately he saw the heavens being torn open and the Spirit descending on him like a dove. And a voice came from heaven, "You are my beloved Son; with you I am well pleased." The Spirit immediately drove him out

into the wilderness. And he was in the wilderness forty days, being tempted by Satan.' (Mark 1:9-13)

We discover that the ministry of Jesus involves

teaching,

   serving,

      healing,

         feeding,

      delivering,

   forgiving

and life-giving.

But, as with the Son of God, it is the Holy Spirit who equips and enables Him to do all those things. Everything He did, He did by the power of the Holy Spirit.

Jesus then commissions His followers to continue His mission. He sends them into the whole world to act as His ambassadors, declaring the glories of the new Kingdom He has initiated. But they can't just pack their bags and leave. Unsurprisingly, they too need the Holy Spirit:

"'For John baptised with water, but you will be baptised with the Holy Spirit not many days from now." So when they had come together, they asked him, "Lord, will you at this time restore the kingdom to Israel?" He said to them: "It is not for you to know the times or seasons the Father has fixed by his own authority. But you will receive power when the Holy Spirit has come upon you; and you will be my witnesses in Jerusalem, and in all Judea and Samaria, and to the ends of the earth."' (Acts 1:5-8)

If Jesus needed the Spirit, how much more do His followers!

GIFTS OF THE SPIRIT

Let's be clear about this: **everyone becomes a Christian only through the work of the Holy Spirit.**

The Holy Spirit gives us the desire and ability to hear and understand the good news.

The Holy Spirit convicts us of our sin and shows us our need for a Saviour.

The Holy Spirit gives us the desire to please the Lord and become more like Christ.

It's the Holy Spirit who changes us.

And it's the Holy Spirit who equips us.

All of this is true for each and every Christian. There are not different categories of Christians, those with the Spirit and those without. Neither can you have a 'bit' of the Spirit. *Every* Christian is Spirit-filled, and gifted to serve the church in particular and the world in general in some way, shape or form.

So, let's look at the gifts listed in the New Testament:

+ Apostle, prophet, teacher, miracles, kinds of healings, helps, administration, tongues (1 Cor. 12:28)

+ Word of wisdom, word of knowledge, faith, gifts of healing, miracles, prophecy, distinguishing between spirits, tongues, interpretation of tongues (1 Cor. 12:8-10)

+ Apostle, prophet, evangelist, pastor-teacher (Eph. 4:11)

+ Prophecy, serving, teaching, encouraging, giving, leadership, mercy (Rom. 12:6-8)

+ Speaking, serving (1 Pet. 4:11)

Again, note that these are *gifts* of the Spirit. We don't earn them. They are not prizes for good behaviour, nor accomplishments. Therefore, there is no room for pride. Even faith itself is a gift, rather than something we accomplish:

 'For by grace you have been saved through faith. And this is your own doing; it is the gift of God, not as a result of works, so that no one may boast.' (Eph. 2:8-9)

Also note that this is not a complete list. At one level, a spiritual gift is nothing more nor less than any ability we have which we put to God's service. My home is a gift from God which I am called to use at the Lord's disposal. Marriage and singleness are gifts from God which we are to use for God's glory and the good of others.

But we can – and should – throw the net even wider. The challenge facing Ronaldo or Messi, if they were Christians, would be how they use their phenomenal gifts as footballers for the glory of God and the service of others.

OKAY, BUT WHAT ABOUT...?

This is all well and good. But you may have noticed that, so far, I have avoided speaking about the gifts that you may be most interested in: things like speaking in tongues, prophecy and healing.

There's good reason for that. Those gifts are controversial, and I wanted to establish some foundational truths about gifts in case we found ourselves unhelpfully distracted by them.

So, whatever you think about what follows, never forget that *all* Christians agree about (1) our total dependency on the Holy Spirit, and (2) that all our service for God is through gifts He has given us. Recognising those truths helps us avoid being judgmental and dismissive of those with whom we disagree.

The Two C's

Christians disagree over what this all means today, so we'll cover the basics of each view.

For the sake of simplicity, there are two main positions when it comes to how we understand several of the spiritual gifts listed in the New Testament. We're talking specifically about some of the more spectacular gifts, like prophecy, tongues, interpretation of tongues, words of knowledge and miracles.

Cessationism is the perspective that some of these gifts have *ceased* since before the end of the first century, when the Apostolic Era ended. The apostles were appointed by God to lay the foundation of the early church, and specifically those who saw Jesus (Paul is considered an apostle because the book of Acts tells us that Jesus appeared to him). Cessationism argues that some or all spiritual gifts, as they define them, have stopped, and are not available for us today.

Continuationism, as you might have guessed, is the view that all the spiritual gifts continue in the Church and are available to Christians today. This is probably the majority view, though there is a wide range of opinion about how we understand the spiritual gifts and how they function.

STOP

What do we think about these two views? What are the strengths and weaknesses of each view?

But even beyond these two views, there's still more to say. For example, we can say prophecy exists, but do we know what prophecy is? We have some general guidelines in 1 Corinthians 14, but how does that help us come to a definition? Does having the 'gift of prophecy' make someone a prophet? Or what about tongues? Are they ordinary languages which the speaker has not learned, or are they out-of-this-world languages, languages of heaven?

There are also questions about cessationism. If, as cessationists generally believe, tongues are human languages that were given at a specific time to help the gospel reach new categories of people, why does Paul imply that he has a private use of tongues, distinct from the use of tongues in the gathered congregation?[5]

These are just a few of the things we don't understand.

I raise these questions not to make a statement, but to illustrate a problem. Just because those questions are real doesn't make continuationism wrong. Equally, we cannot simply dismiss cessationists as Spirit-suppressing sceptics!

THE GREATEST OF THESE IS LOVE

This debate has raged for centuries and continues to divide Christians. There are sincere Christians on both sides who are firmly convinced that they believe what they believe because that's what the Bible teaches. Both can't be right, can they? But both may be wrong, at least in their more extreme expressions.

It can be no accident that the two chapters on gifts and gospel spirituality in 1 Corinthians sandwich the famous chapter on love, which begins with these words: *'If I speak in the tongues of*

---

5   See 1 Corinthians 14:18-19.

men and of angels, but have not love, I am a noisy gong or a clanging cymbal.[6]

Please do keep in mind that you can be a devout follower of Jesus and hold to either view. You can take the Bible seriously whilst holding to either view. This is not a primary, first-order doctrine – it is possible for genuine believers to have different views on the gifts of the Spirit today and still hold to the fundamental doctrines of Christianity.

So we must approach our brothers and sisters who believe differently with humility and love. Let's be eager to count others more significant than ourselves.[7] Let's be determined to encourage and be encouraged in the gospel, so that we provoke and are provoked to love and good works.

MEMORY VERSE

'For by the grace given to me I say to everyone among you not to think of himself more highly than he ought.' (Rom. 12:3)

SUMMARY

The Holy Spirit gives us faith to believe the gospel of Christ. He empowers us to serve God and His church through specific gifts given to each member of the body of Christ: these are spiritual gifts. We are totally dependent on the Holy Spirit, and all our service for God is through the gifts He has given us, for God's glory alone!

WHAT'S THE POINT?

To figure out your gifts, get busy serving.

8. HOW DO I KNOW WHAT MY GIFTS ARE?

RECAP

We're nearing the end of our exploration of service and Christian discipleship. I hope that two main ideas are at the front of your mind: 1) God made us to serve Him and others; 2) God is the Hero, the ultimate servant who laid down His life for us and empowers all our service. We are useless servants apart from Him.

In the last chapter, we talked about spiritual gifts. This might leave you wondering about your own spiritual gifts – how has the Holy Spirit equipped you to serve the body of Christ? If you don't know, how do you begin figuring it out? Should you figure it out?

JAMES

James has become very interested in talking about the gifts of the Holy Spirit. He's very keen to learn which of the gifts he has, so he comes to you asking if there is some special test that he can take to find out.

QUIZ CULTURE

If you're on social media, you've probably clicked through one of those personality quizzes: 'Which Superhero Are You?', 'What Does Your Favourite Colour Say About You?' or even 'Who's Your

Famous Movie Character Soulmate?[1] I know they're rubbish…
yet it's all too easy to play along. After all, who doesn't want to find
out about their inner superhero?

> **STOP**
>
> *Why do you think these quizzes are so interesting to us? Have you ever
> been drawn into one – if so, what was attractive about it?*

My guess is that our quiz culture is just another expression of our
self-love, our narcissism. We want to see ourselves in a new and
better light ('it says I'm like Spiderman!') and, ideally, advertise
our sparkling selves on social media for all our friends to admire.
This confirms all that we want to be true about ourselves: we're
unique, smart, attractive, witty, thoughtful.

Now don't get me wrong: God *did* create each one of us as unique
image bearers – every person *is* stunningly and wonderfully made
with individual strengths, created to love and serve, and so glorify
God!

Our problem is that we quickly focus in on ourselves, and begin
to believe that we must do something to earn God's kindness.
What should be a simple, childlike gratitude for God's good
gifts mutates into self-satisfaction faster than Superman gets his
underpants on over his tights.

NO REALLY, IT'S NOT ABOUT US!

Okay, but what does all this have to do with spiritual gifts? Well,
our tendency to gaze at ourselves doesn't stop with Facebook
quizzes.

Of course, it's not selfish, in and of itself, to want to understand
more about how God made us. And it's not at all a bad desire to

---

1   Seriously!   http://www.zimbio.com/quiz/KOkoJPbyWBx/Famous+
Movie+Character+Soulmate accessed on 5th September, 2017.

want to figure out the gifts God has given us to serve His Church. But there *is* a wrong way to go about it: when we make it all about us. I know my own heart, and I know this is exactly what I tend to do and be like.

Next time you're at your laptop, Google 'spiritual gifts' and you'll find a ton of books and resources dedicated to helping you find your spiritual gifts. You'll find online quizzes and tests promising to tell you your unique gift and usher you into a new era of powerful service and blessing.

> **STOP**
>
> *What's the problem with this kind of spiritual gift search?*

When we're digging deep to discover our spiritual gifts, what (or who) are we thinking about? Essentially, we're thinking about *us*. That should be enough to raise alarm bells because we know that God is the Hero of our story. It's good to rehearse the truth that *whoever it's about, it's not about me!*

Let's look at Romans 12:3-8 again:

'For by the grace given to me I say to everyone among you not to think of himself more highly than he ought to think, but to think with sober judgment, each according to the measure of faith that God has assigned. For as in one body we have many members, and the members do not all have the same function, so we, though many, are one body in Christ, and individually members one of another. Having gifts that differ according to the grace given to us, let us use them: if prophecy, in proportion to our faith; if service, in our serving; the one who teaches, in his teaching; the one who exhorts, in his exhortation; the one who contributes, in generosity; the one who leads, with zeal; the one who does acts of mercy, with cheerfulness.'

Interestingly, in verse 6, Paul assumes believers will know what their spiritual gifts are. He simply tells them to use whatever their gifts are in an appropriate way.

When the apostle Peter writes about gifts to Christians scattered around what is now Turkey, he simply tells them how to use their gifts, but doesn't see the need to encourage them to find out what they are: *'As each has received a gift, use it to serve one another as good stewards of God's varied grace.'* (1 Pet. 4:10)

It might seem as if Paul and Peter skipped a step. How can these believers use their gifts without knowing how they are gifted?

JAMES

I'm confused. How do I find out what my spiritual gift is?

STOP

How do we help James answer this question in a way that is both biblical and helpful?

WHICH CAME FIRST?

This raises a question: do we need to discover our gifts to serve, or do we need to serve to discover our gifts?

John Piper writes that our main problem, over and above not *knowing* our gifts, is that we don't really care about the very purpose for which the gifts are given, namely, building up others:

'I really believe that the problem of not knowing our spiritual gifts is not a basic problem. More basic is the problem of not desiring very much to strengthen other people's faith.'[2]

---

2   John   Piper,   http://www.desiringgod.org/messages/spiritual-gifts, accessed on 1st September, 2017.

The answer to that 'which came first' question is 'neither'! The aim of all our activity is to love the Lord and to love His people. The core intention of any Spirit-empowered service is to strengthen the faith of our brothers and sisters.

This draws a line under it, doesn't it?

> Rather than asking what our gifts are, here's a better question: 'how can I serve my local church?'

> Rather than asking what our gifts are, we should ask: 'How can I strengthen and encourage those around me today? How can I help others to delight in Jesus, to grow in grace and in the knowledge of the Saviour?'

This is what it means to use the gifts of the Spirit in building up the church.

STOP

How can you get on with strengthening the faith of those around you? Think of a few specific people and come up with some ideas about how you can encourage them in the Lord. Also think about ways in which you can serve your church. Now put it into practice!

PRACTICAL SERVING

If you're still not sure about your spiritual gifts, ask your church leaders how you can help. What's needed in your church? Ask your mates how you can pray for them. Keep your eyes open when your church gathers – are there people who look lonely or sad? Is there anyone hanging around the edges with whom you could strike up a conversation? Are there jobs that need doing – setting up chairs, looking after children, washing up cups?

We discover and use the gifts God gives us as we rush to serve our church, as we remind our brothers and sisters about Jesus, and as we point those who don't know Christ to our great Saviour.

So, rather than spending those ten minutes filling out a questionnaire all about your own habits, preferences and behaviours, take the time to humble yourself before God in prayer and offer your life for His service and His glory. He will take you up on it. Guaranteed!

STOP

Look at our Romans passage again. You might notice something interesting: serving is considered a gift. But wait – aren't all Christians called to serve others? What's going on here?

I LIKE TO SERVE...BUT DO I HAVE THE 'GIFT OF SERVICE'?

Yes, it's still true that all Christians are called to serve. This is not your get-out clause! But it's described in Romans 12:7 as a gift because there are some who seem to excel at it. Service seems to come more easily to them because they are particularly gifted by God to serve. The same goes with giving, and being merciful. These are behaviours which every Christian should demonstrate, but in which some excel.

Can you see why God has done it this way?

 ILLUSTRATION

Think about learning to use a computer. There are at least a couple of ways to go about it. You could just sit in front of one and find your way around in a long process of trial and error. Or you could sit beside someone who knows a thing or two about computers and watch as she does her magic. That way, you watch which button to press, where to point the cursor, how to cut and paste and so on. You then swap seats and she encourages you, reminds you, helps you and gets you up to speed. In other words, we learn best by being shown and then doing it alongside the person showing us, before being left to get on with it on our own.

So it is with giving, for example. Identify someone in your church who seems particularly generous with their time, their possessions, their money. Watch them, and ask them questions about it. What motivates them, how do they keep going, how do they know the best way to express their generosity? You may never become as good at giving as them, but you will certainly become a better giver. And you may actually find out that you too have that gift because of the enjoyment you find in giving and blessing others.

So, whatever it is that you do, do it well and enthusiastically. That's how you'll find out what your specific gifts are.

That doesn't mean that you don't do other things! For instance, someone might be gifted as a teacher, but that does not give them permission to look away when mercy is needed. It means simply that you can invest in and excel at those gifts that the Lord seems to use to impact, bless, encourage and strengthen others.

STAND FIRM

In all these things, keep in mind that the point of spiritual gifts is to strengthen our brothers and sisters in their faith in Jesus. Think about the world in which we live and the sin that continues to plague us, and you can see how important this is. We desperately need one another if we are to stand firm in Jesus and resist temptation from the world, our flesh and the devil. Flip just a few pages on from Paul's instructions to the Corinthian church about spiritual gifts and you'll find him leaving that same church with this final instruction:

'Be watchful, stand firm in the faith, act like men, be strong. Let all that you do be done in love.' (1 Cor. 16:13-14)

They would not need to be commanded to 'stand firm in the faith' if they weren't prone to wobble. The same is true of us! Our wandering hearts tend toward doubt and unbelief. So let's actively seek to strengthen one another in the Lord. Look for areas in which your brothers and sisters might be struggling to trust God, and come alongside them to help them stand firm. This is the power of the Spirit in you, equipping you to love and build up the Body of Christ. This is what Spirit-empowered ministry and service looks like.

 MEMORY VERSE

'As each has received a gift, use it to serve one another, as good stewards of God's varied grace.' (1 Pet. 4:10)

 SUMMARY

Instead of looking inward to discover your spiritual gifts, dig deep into serving your local church. It is in the process of serving that your gifts will become more and more clear. Our ultimate desire should be to strengthen the faith of our brothers and sisters in Jesus, and to point the lost to our beautiful Saviour!

WHAT'S THE POINT?

Our gifts are for strengthening the church – now and for eternity.

9. PUTTING MY GIFTS TO WORK

RECAP

We have covered several aspects of service as a follower of Jesus. Hopefully the main theme in your mind is that God is the Hero – we serve because He first served us! He not only made us and saved us so that we will serve; He also empowers us by His Spirit to serve His church. All the good we do is because of Him, and we do no good apart from Him! Let's enjoy this truth now as we think about putting our gifts to work.

Our final chapter is about getting on with it. We've seen that spiritual gifts are given by the Holy Spirit for strengthening the body of Christ. But before we unpack more of what it might look like to use our gifts, it will be helpful to dive more deeply into why we need them.

JAMES

James comes to talk to you about some people he's been talking to online about the spiritual gifts. 'They say you're holding me back. That I need to have the power of the Holy Spirit released into my life to become the best that I can be. They say that I am missing the blessing of Holy Spirit power. Is that true?'

STOP

How do we answer James' question?

WHY DO WE HAVE GIFTS OF THE SPIRIT?

Consider these two passages from Paul's letter to the church in Rome:

1. Romans 1:11-12

'For I long to see you, that I may impart to you some spiritual gift to strengthen you – that is, that we may be mutually encouraged by each other's faith, both yours and mine.'

Paul sees spiritual gifts as a means of strengthening the believers in Rome.

Notice that he doesn't have any particular gifts in mind.

The phrase *'some spiritual gift'* is deliberately vague. His ambition is simply that they might be strengthened and encouraged through his ministry. This could look different depending on the situation: perhaps as Paul taught the Bible someone was challenged to think about using their home more, and so learning how to excel in the gift of hospitality. Or maybe Paul spoke to someone and suggested they join him on a mission trip to learn how to explain the gospel to people. But notice, in verse 12, that it is two-way traffic: Paul will be both a beneficiary and a benefactor. He will be blessed and be a blessing. That's how it always works in the kingdom of God!

2. Romans 12:3-8

'For by the grace given to me I say to everyone among you not to think of himself more highly than he ought to think, but to think with sober judgment, each according to the measure of faith that God has assigned. For as in one body we have many members, and the members do not all have the same function, so we, though many, are one body in Christ, and individually members of one another. Having gifts that differ according to the grace given to us, let us use them: if prophecy, in proportion to our faith; if service, in our serving; the one who teaches, in his teaching; the one who exhorts, in his exhortation;

the one who contributes, in generosity; the one who leads, with zeal; the one who does acts of mercy, with cheerfulness.'

As individual Christians, we all belong to a larger group. Gifts are given to help us contribute to that group and build up others in that group. It is impossible to overstate the significance of the phrase Paul uses: *each member belongs to all the others.* Isn't that startling – and scary!

Most of us are okay with acknowledging that we belong to the Lord, but we're a little less sure when we read that we *belong* to each other. It cramps my style and robs me of my sense of personal freedom. Too right, says Paul! Paul is referring to a local church. He cannot think for a moment about being a Christian and not belonging to a church. In that church, we all contribute and we all benefit.

The local church is the primary context for the use of our gifts.

Notice that I said *primary* context. It's not the only context, by any means. Our gifts ought to be a blessing to others, whoever they are. A gift of administration (yes, it does exist; see 1 Corinthians 12:28...but hold your excitement!) can be used to bless others by running a drop-in centre for the homeless. Paul helps us make this distinction in Galatians 6:10 (NIV), when he writes: *'As we have opportunity, let us do good to all people, especially to those who belong to the family of believers.'* So use whatever talents and abilities you have for the good of everyone you can, but make sure you do so with other Christians in mind.

MANY PARTS, ONE BODY

Imagine a body with all toes and no fingers. Or three noses and no eyes. Strange things happen, of course, but we would all know it shouldn't be that way. Our bodies are precisely designed so that each body part contributes to the functioning of the whole. One nose is enough, and both eyes are needed for maximum vision. This is why Paul uses this illustration to talk about spiritual gifts to a divided and bickering Corinthian church:

'If the whole body were an eye, where would be the sense of hearing? If the whole body were an ear, where would be the sense of smell? But as it is, God arranged the members in the body, each one of them, as he chose. If all were a single member, where would the body be? As it is, there are many parts, yet one body.

The eye cannot say to the hand, "I have no need of you," nor again the head to the feet, "I have no need of you." On the contrary, the parts of the body that seem to be weaker are indispensable, and on those parts of the body that we think less honourable we bestow the greater honour, and our unpresentable parts are treated with greater modesty, which our more presentable parts do not require. But God has so composed the body, giving greater honour to the part that lacked it, that there may be no division in the body, but that the members may have the same care for one another. If one member suffers, all suffer together; if one member is honoured, all rejoice together. Now you are the body of Christ and individually members of it.' (1 Cor. 12:17-27)

Can you see a theme here? Like the passage in Romans, Paul is hammering home the glorious truth that each member of the body of Christ is essential for the whole. *That means you!* There is not one tiny body part that is not needed by the whole body, and the same holds true in the church. We are, after all, the Body of Christ!

BLESSED TO SERVE

Our individualistic society wants to make everything about *me* – something is meaningful if it moves *me*; a gift is valuable if it matters to *me*. But if we're part of the body of Christ, then following Jesus means we're concerned about both Him and others! When one part of the body makes itself greater than the rest it has the cancerous effect of destroying the body.

We must look at spiritual gifts through the lens of the church, or we will end up making it all about us and so creating division in the one body of Christ.

Let's break this down a bit: spiritual gifts are not *for* us as individuals. They're certainly not for our own power, position or popularity. There are false teachers who have used so-called spiritual gifts to bring glory and wealth to themselves. The root of this sin is no different than the root of all sin: we want to be God. We want the power and glory that belongs only to the Lord.

It's easy to see this played out in so many churches all over the world. For example, someone has the gift of teaching/preaching.

People get saved through their ministry.

Their church starts to grow.

Services are packed out.

The Lord has used gifted preachers and teachers through the centuries – men like Charles Spurgeon and Martyn Lloyd-Jones. But that gift can so easily become twisted and inverted. It can quickly become all about the preacher, and the pulpit can become a platform for him to strut his stuff. People become useful only so long as they massage the preacher's ego.

But the Bible makes it clear that anything we have been given – any strength, any ability, any wealth, any blessing, any resource, anything at all – we have received *from* God and *for* the encouragement and building up and strengthening of God's people. We need to continue remembering that *whoever it's about, it's not about me!*

That's why it makes good sense to have a couple of chapters on spiritual gifts in a book about serving. At its simplest definition, spiritual gifts are *for* service. We are gloriously, beautifully and sufficiently empowered to serve one another, so that together we bring God the Father glory as we make God the Son known through the power of God the Spirit.

And that is our great hope! We serve others for the fame of Jesus *through the power given by the Holy Spirit.* Our role in the body of Christ does not depend on us, but on the power of the one who works powerfully in us and through us.

PUTTING OUR GIFTS TO USE – HOW WILL WE WAKE UP TOMORROW?

John Piper brings this all home by focusing our vision on the practical reality of how we live.

How will we wake up tomorrow?

What will be our desire and aim?

'*...the basic problem is becoming the kind of person who wakes up in the morning, thanks God for our great salvation, and then says, "Lord, O how I want to strengthen people's faith today. Grant that at the end of this day somebody will be more confident of your promises and more joyful in your grace because I crossed his path."*'[1]

This is a no-brainer, isn't it? Having that kind of attitude and view on life is far more appealing than being taken up and consumed by 'me.'

---

1   John Piper, http://www.desiringgod.org/messages/spiritual-gifts, accessed on 1st September, 2017.

But this is nothing new. It has been the theme of our book. More significantly, it will be the theme of eternity. Life in the New Creation that God is bringing in will be a life of devoted, thankful, humble and enthusiastic service. No one ever gets promoted above the rank of a servant because there is no higher rank.

A life of glad service here and now prepares us for a life of glad service in eternity. And when I think about it like that, I get all pumped up to go out and serve. After all, that's not just what Jesus did. That is who Jesus is!

MEMORY VERSE

'Whatever you do, work heartily, as for the Lord and not for men.'
(Col. 3:23)

SUMMARY

Each and every believer is part of Christ's body. We belong to one another, and the gifts we've been given are vitally important for the health of the whole body. So our prayer and aim is that we wake up each day with the desire to strengthen the faith of our brothers and sisters. We look forward to our glorious future – an eternal life of service with our redeemed family and the Servant King who served us by saving us from our sin.

Also available in the *First Steps series* …

This series of short workbooks, from the 9Marks series, are designed to help you think through some of life's big questions.

1. GOD: Is He Out There?

2. WAR: Why Did Life Just Get Harder?

3. VOICES: Who Am I Listening To?

4. BIBLE: Can We Trust It?

5. BELIEVE: What Should I Know?

6. CHARACTER: How Do I Change?

7. TRAINING: How Do I Grow As A Christian?

8. CHURCH: Do I Have To Go?

9. RELATIONSHIPS: How Do I Make Things Right?

10. SERVICE: How Do I Give Back?

GOD: Is He Out There?

978-1-5271-0296-5

WAR: Why Did Life Just Get Harder?

978-1-5271-0297-2

VOICES: Who Am I Listening To?

978-1-5271-0298-9

BIBLE: Can We Trust It?

978-1-5271-0000-8

BELIEVE: What Should I Know?

978-1-5271-0305-4

CHARACTER: How Do I Change?

978-1-5271-0101-2

TRAINING: How Do I
Grow As A Christian?

978-1-5271-0102-9

CHURCH: Do I Have To
Go?

978-1-5271-0426-6

RELATIONSHIPS: How Do I
Make Things Right?

978-1-5271-0471-6

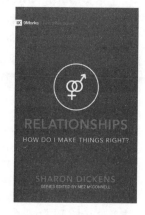

IX 9Marks

Building Healthy Churches

9Marks exists to equip church leaders with a biblical vision and practical resources for displaying God's glory to the nations through healthy churches.

To that end, we want to see churches characterized by these nine marks of health:

1 Expositional Preaching
2 Biblical Theology
3 A Biblical Understanding of the Gospel
4 A Biblical Understanding of Conversion
5 A Biblical Understanding of Evangelism
6 Biblical Church Membership
7 Biblical Church Discipline
8 Biblical Discipleship
9 Biblical Church Leadership

Find more titles at

www.9Marks.org

Gospel Churches for Scotland's Poorest

20schemes exists to bring gospel hope to Scotland's poorest communities through the revitalisation and planting of healthy, gospel-preaching churches, ultimately led by a future generation of indigenous church leaders.

> *'If we are really going to see a turnaround in the lives of residents in our poorest communities, then we have to embrace a radical and long-term strategy which will bring gospel-hope to untold thousands.'*

MEZ McCONNELL, Ministry Director

We believe that building healthy churches in Scotland's poorest communities will bring true, sustainable, and long-term renewal to countless lives.

THE NEED IS URGENT

Learn more about our work and how to partner with us at:

20SCHEMES.COM
TWITTER.COM/20SCHEMES
FACEBOOK.COM/20SCHEMES
INSTAGRAM.COM/20SCHEMES

Christian Focus Publications

Our mission statement —

STAYING FAITHFUL

In dependence upon God we seek to impact the world through literature faithful to His infallible Word, the Bible. Our aim is to ensure that the Lord Jesus Christ is presented as the only hope to obtain forgiveness of sin, live a useful life and look forward to heaven with Him.

Our books are published in four imprints:

CHRISTIAN
FOCUS

Popular works including bi-ographies, commentaries, basic doctrine and Christian living.

CHRISTIAN
HERITAGE

Books representing some of the best material from the rich heritage of the church.

MENTOR

Books written at a level suitable for Bible College and seminary students, pastors, and other seri-ous readers. The imprint includes commentaries, doctrinal studies, examination of current issues and church history.

CF4•K

Children's books for quality Bible teaching and for all age groups: Sunday school curriculum, puzzle and activity books; personal and family devotional titles, biographies and inspirational stories — because you are never too young to know Jesus!

Christian Focus Publications Ltd,
Geanies House, Fearn, Ross-shire,
IV20 1TW, Scotland, United Kingdom.
www.christianfocus.com